TOP 10
SPORTS
★ STARS ★

BASKETBALL'S
TOP 10 SLAM DUNKERS

Ken Rappoport

Enslow Publishers, Inc.
40 Industrial Road
Box 398
Berkeley Heights, NJ 07922
USA

http://www.enslow.com

Library of Congress Cataloging-in-Publication Data

Rappoport, Ken.

    Basketball's top 10 slam dunkers / Ken Rappoport.
        p. cm. — (Top 10 sports stars)
    Includes bibliographical references and index.
    Summary: "A collective biography of the top 10 slam dunkers, both past and present, which includes accounts of game action, career statistics, and more"—Provided by publisher.
    ISBN 978-0-7660-3467-9
    1. Basketball players—United States—Biography—Juvenile literature. 2. Basketball players—Rating of—United States—Juvenile literature. I. Title. II. Title: Basketball top ten slam dunkers.
    GV884.A1R35 2010
    796.3230922—dc22
    [B]

                          2009027172

052011 Lake Book Manufacturing, Inc., Melrose Park, IL

Printed in the United States of America

10 9 8 7 6 5 4 3 2

To Our Readers: We have done our best to make sure all Internet addresses in this book were active and appropriate when we went to press. However, the author and the publisher have no control over and assume no liability for the material available on those Internet sites or on other Web sites they may link to. Any comments or suggestions can be sent by e-mail to comments@enslow.com or to the address on the back cover.

♻ Enslow Publishers, Inc., is committed to printing our books on recycled paper. The paper in every book contains 10% to 30% post-consumer waste (PCW). The cover board on the outside of each book contains 100% PCW. Our goal is to do our part to help young people and the environment too!

Illustration Credits: All photos courtesy Associated Press/Wide World Photos, except pp. 14 and 17, NBAE/Getty Images; p.18, Manny Millan/Sports Illustrated/Getty Images; and p. 21, Focus on Sport/Getty Images.

Cover Illustration: Associated Press/Wide World Photos

TOP 10

CONTENTS

I magine if there was no LeBron James powering to the basket. No Shaquille O'Neal splintering backboards. No Vince Carter rattling the rim with his "Tomahawk Slam" dunk shot.

No National Basketball Associaton—no NBA.

If not for James Naismith, that could very well be a possibility. In the early 1890s, Dr. Naismith was a physical education instructor at a school in Springfield, Massachusetts. To keep his students occupied over the winter months, he made up a new game.

He nailed up a peach basket at each end of the gym and handed his kids a soccer ball. Delighted, they scrambled around the court attempting to toss the ball into the baskets. Thus the game of "basketball" was born.

Now imagine this: Dr. Naismith taking a time-traveling car to the present day. Naismith would be stunned to see what the future held for his game.

His invention had evolved into a billion-dollar industry. Not only were NBA games shown on national television and followed by millions in America, but basketball had become an international passion.

Basketball's Top 10 Slam Dunkers pays tribute to those players who have raised the game to new levels with their creativity. Because of their unique talents, some forced rule changes or changed the way the game was played.

As the star of the Cleveland Cavaliers, LeBron James is a "small forward" who plays big—at more than one position. He is among the new "hybrid" players who can do it all.

Shaquille O'Neal, one of the strongest players in NBA history, has been a force to reckon with ever since his early days with the Orlando Magic. Four NBA titles tell the story.

And Vince Carter's dazzling dunks have seen their time on many ESPN highlight shows through the years.

Here are other all-time greats you will meet in *Basketball's Top 10 Slam Dunkers*:

Julius Erving, who seemed to walk on air and opened a new pathway to dunk shooting; Kareem Abdul-Jabbar, the NBA's all-time leading scorer who forced rule changes because of his domination in the paint; Dominique Wilkins, who won two NBA Slam-Dunk Contests; Hakeem Olajuwon, who was one of the league's most athletic centers; Darryl Dawkins, a man of many dunk shots who called himself "Chocolate Thunder"; Bill Russell, the Boston Celtics great who won eleven NBA titles; and Michael Jordan, whom some call the greatest of all time.

And to think, it all started with a Phys Ed instructor and a peach basket.

KAREEM ABDUL-JABBAR

KAREEM
ABDUL-JABBAR

The Los Angeles Lakers'

Kareem Abdul-Jabbar was

determined to change history.

Since playing in Minneapolis, the Lakers
franchise had never beaten the Boston Celtics
in eight championship playoff meetings.
Would 1985 finally be the year?
The Lakers led the Celtics three games to

never lost one to the Lakers. And Boston has never lost one to Kareem Abdul-Jabbar."[1]

Jabbar, even as a teenager, made an immediate impact wherever he played. He led Power Memorial High School to three straight New York City Catholic championships. At that time he was known as Lew Alcindor before he adopted the Muslim name of Kareem Abdul-Jabbar.

Alcindor led UCLA to national championships in 1967, 1968, and 1969 and a remarkable 88–2 record. Can you imagine a player being so dominant that he caused college basketball rules to be changed? The dunk shot, which was one of Alcindor's favorite weapons, was ruled illegal in his time at UCLA. Alcindor develped his famous "sky hook" shot to make up for his dunk shot.

In the NBA, he teamed with Oscar Robertson and led the Milwaukee Bucks to an NBA-best 66–16 record and the league championship in just his second season in the NBA. Alcindor was the Finals MVP.

When the 1970–71 season ended, Alcindor adopted the Muslim name of Kareem Abdul-Jabbar. He had been a Muslim since his days at UCLA.

Jabbar was traded to Los Angeles in 1975. Jabbar and Magic Johnson teamed up to make the Lakers the most dominant NBA team of the '80s. Still no win over the Celtics.

Game 6 of the 1985 Finals—Celtics vs. Lakers. The teams were tied 55–55 at the half. Then the Lakers took over the game, making six straight shots at the start of the third quarter. By the end of the period, Los Angeles led 82–73.

With 2:27 left in the game, Jabbar hit a turnaround jumper in the lane. Twenty-nine seconds later, he connected with his patented "sky hook." And with 61 seconds remaining, he scored on a fourteen-foot jumper.

Jabbar was on his way to the bench with 14 seconds left, and the Lakers were on their way to a 111–100 victory.

Jabbar couldn't hide his feelings. The goggled 7-foot-2 Lakers center waved both index fingers in a "Number One" gesture as he walked off the court.

The Lakers had finally beaten the Celtics. Jabbar would go on to win a total of six MVP awards to go along with six NBA championships. For Jabbar, the 1985 victory over the Celtics topped them all.

KAREEM ABDUL-JABBAR

BORN: April 16, 1946, New York City.

HIGH SCHOOL: Power Memorial, New York City.

COLLEGE: UCLA.

PROS: Milwaukee Bucks, 1969–75; Los Angeles Lakers, 1975–89.

HONORS: 1967–68, USBWA College Player of the Year; 1969 Naismith Award; NBA Rookie of the Year, 1970; six-time NBA Most Valuable Player; two-time Finals MVP; Hall of Fame, 1995.

Kareem Abdul-Jabbar   **9**

VINCE CARTER

VINCE CARTER

Vince Carter was excited. Dunks were one of his favorite things to do. It was one week before the 2000 NBA All-Star Game, and he was going to compete in the Slam Dunk Contest.

But there was a problem. A week before the All-Star weekend in Oakland, Carter had a finger injury. After a visit to the doctor, Vince had stitches and sported a bandage on his left hand.

But it wasn't going to stop him from competing in the Slam-Dunk Contest. His dunk routine was all set. But on his way to the arena, Carter decided to try something new.

He was always trying something new. He had started young, when he was in sixth grade. A bunch of kids were over at the outside courts at the Ormand Beach

Middle School in Florida. They were trying to dunk a tennis ball or volleyball in the basket. Carter was 5-foot-7, so he decided to try dunking a basketball.

"I threw the ball up, went off of one leg, jumped, and got it with one hand. Believe me, it was amazing," Carter remembered.[1]

In high school, all he wanted to do was dunk. "Dr. J," Julius Erving, was his role model. When he saw a "crazy dunk" on the ESPN highlights, Carter would try to imitate it.[2]

At the University of North Carolina, Carter continued his dunk-shooting exploits. As a Tar Heel, Carter earned national attention on ESPN's Sport Center and a cover shot on *Sports Illustrated* with his incredible dunks.

Carter started his NBA career in 1998 with the Toronto Raptors. He was selected as the Rookie of the Year. The following year, Carter was selected for the All-Star game the first time.

Time for the 2000 Slam Dunk Contest. By then, Carter had shrugged off his finger injury. Taking the ball from dunk partner Tracy McGrady on the bounce, Carter shuffled it between his legs and rattled the boards with his newly patented "Tomahawk Slam."

Other creative dunks followed: a "360-degree Windmill," a "between-the-legs," and an "elbow dunk." The arena rocked with the fans' thunderous applause.

"I saw something like it in a magazine," Carter said, "the guy jumping through the air and putting (the ball) through his legs. I wondered if I could do that with a bounce."[3] It was no contest. Carter was declared the NBA's slam-dunk champion.

Although Carter doesn't like to rank his slam dunks, he

does recall one particular shot as his all-time favorite. Carter was playing for the United States national team against France in the 2000 Summer Olympics in Sydney, Australia. It was four minutes into the second half when Carter intercepted a pass about thirty feet from the basket. Only one player stood between Carter and a score—France's 7-foot-2 center Frederic Weis. A step or two into the foul line, Carter went straight into the air. Up, up, and up. He spread his legs as he leaped over his opponent, who was nearly a foot taller. Carter's dunk shot swept through the net and rattled the backboard.

"That was a 10, or a 12," marveled USA teammate Tim Hardaway. "I've never seen anyone jump over a 7-footer."[4] The play was later referred to as "le dunk de la mort," or "the dunk of death."

VINCE CARTER

BORN: January 26, 1977, Daytona Beach, Florida.

. . . .

COLLEGE: North Carolina.

. . . .

PRO: Toronto Raptors, 1998–2004; New Jersey Nets, 2005–2009; Orlando Magic, 2009–present.

. . . .

AWARDS: Eight-time NBA All-Star, two-time All-NBA selection, 1999 Rookie of the Year, 2000 NBA Slam Dunk champion.

. . . .

DARRYL DAWKINS

DARRYL
DAWKINS

All eyes were on Darryl Dawkins as the Philadelphia 76ers took the floor to face the San Antonio Spurs on December 6, 1979.

Would he do it again? Just three weeks earlier, on November 13 in Kansas City, it had happened. The 76ers' center was going up for a dunk shot.

Pat Williams, the 76ers' general manager, said, "I've seen Darryl make that move every week, every game. There was nothing unusual about it."[1]

This time was different. When Darryl went up, the backboard went down. BAM! It sounded like a bomb went off. The glass came showering down. Glass flew everywhere, nicking players and getting into the hair of others.

Dawkins didn't know what was happening. "I ran out of there faster than anyone," he recalled of his backboard-breaking shot.[2]

Now Dawkins didn't break the backboard viciously. He enjoyed entertaining, and he would try to make his dunks super special. In fact, he had a name for each of them. How did that start?

Dawkins was playing in a game early in his career when he dunked on an opponent. "I turned to him and said, 'Yo Mama.' We just started laughing." After the game, a reporter asked what the dunk was called. "Yo Mama" was the answer.[3]

"I just started giving them names after that."[4]

Some of the dunks that followed: The Rim Wrecker. The Go-Rilla. The Spine Chiller Supreme. The Look Out Below. The Cover Your Head.

The backboard incident in Kansas City was the talk of the league for many days. As Dawkins went through warm-ups with his teammates three weeks later to face the Spurs, a buzz went through the crowd.

First quarter, Dawkins rocked the rim, but the backboard held up. Same thing second quarter. And the third. Finally, it was the fourth quarter, and the 76ers were running away from the Spurs. With 6 minutes and 42 seconds remaining, it happened. Dawkins went up for a dunk shot . . . and brought the hoop crashing down with him!

The power of Dawkins' shot had knocked the basket rim clean off and sent a shower of glass spilling onto the court. Dawkins was the only player under the basket and managed to escape unhurt. Dawkins became an instant celebrity.

The league soon ruled that a player who broke backboards in the future would be fined and suspended. The league also installed "breakaway" rims in all its courts to prevent such future mishaps.

With his size and strength, the 6-foot-11, 252-pound Dawkins was a powerful force and one of the NBA's most entertaining and popular players. Over fourteen seasons, Dawkins averaged 12 points and 6 rebounds and participated in 109 playoff games.

DARRYL DAWKINS

BORN: January 11, 1957, Orlando, Florida.

· ·

HIGH SCHOOL: Maynard Evans High
School, Orlando, Florida.

· ·

COLLEGE: Southern Methodist University.

· ·

PRO: Philadelphia 76ers, 1975–82; New
Jersey Nets, 1982–88; Detroit Pistons,
1987–88; Utah Jazz, 1988–89.

· ·

JULIUS ERVING

JULIUS ERVING

They had a red, white, and blue basketball. They had a 3-point shot. They had a free-wheeling, faster tempo. And they had Julius Erving.

In the late 1960s, the American Basketball Association (ABA) was a maverick league ready to take on the established NBA. It was a volatile time in basketball, and Erving—nicknamed "Dr. J"—was about to change the sport forever.

The ABA and NBA were about as different as leagues could be. The long-established NBA featured a conservative style with an emphasis on strong team play. The upstart ABA featured an up-tempo, fast-break game and dunks with an emphasis on individual flair.

Erving just loved the ABA style of play. At the

University of Massachusetts, he averaged 26.3 points and 20.2 rebounds in two varsity seasons—but dunking was forbidden under college rules. Erving left school after his junior year to sign with the ABA's Virginia Squires.

Getting ready for his first ABA game, Erving felt confident that he could rebound with the best. But could he score? The big men in the ABA were intimidating. Erving worried about whether he could dunk over seasoned pros who were much taller. The 6-foot-7 Erving didn't have long to find out.

Driving to the hoop, Erving saw two huge obstacles in his way—the Kentucky Colonels' 7-2 Artis Gilmore and 6-9 Dan Issel. Leaping into the air with all his might, Erving went between the two defenders, who were reaching up to stop him. He felt himself hanging in the air beyond their reach.

"Then I dunked on them so hard, I fell on my back," Erving said. "Just doing that made me confident to go after anyone, anytime, anywhere, without any fear."[1]

Erving thrived in this environment. Word of his creative, entertaining dunks spread. While playing for five years in the ABA with Virginia and New York, Erving won three scoring titles, three MVP awards, and two league titles. Financial problems eventually caused the ABA to fold. Four teams survived to join the NBA.

The NBA took a page from the ABA book by marketing individual players. Like the ABA, the NBA became a star-driven league. With the advent of big-money TV contracts, the stars joined the league in becoming rich. The NBA also adopted the Slam Dunk Contest, the 3-point shot, shoe endorsements, and giveaways for the fans.

Because of a contract dispute, the New York Nets were forced to sell Erving to the Philadelphia 76ers. During his eleven years in the NBA, Erving was an all-star each season and the MVP in 1981. One play typified Erving's talents.

It was the fourth game of the 1980 NBA Finals between Philadelphia and the Los Angeles Lakers. Erving, normally a forward, was playing backcourt as the final minutes ticked down. Erving brought the ball upcourt and drove past defender Mark Landsberger trying for a layup. But Kareem Abdul-Jabbar, the Lakers' 7-foot center, suddenly forced Erving behind the backboard. With the ball cradled in one hand, Erving reached out and around the Lakers' center and put in an underhand shot for a basket.

An incredible play—all in a day's work for basketball's trailblazing player.

JULIUS ERVING

BORN: February 22, 1950, Roosevelt, NY.

HIGH SCHOOL: Roosevelt High School.

COLLEGE: University of Massachusetts.

PRO: Virginia Squires, 1971–73; New York Nets, 1973–76; Philadelphia 76ers, 1976–87.

HONORS: ABA Most Valuable Player, 1974, 1976; five-time ABA All-Star; NBA Most Valuable Player, 1981; *Sporting News* NBA MVP, 1981; All-NBA First Team, 1978, 1980–83; two-time NBA All-Star Game MVP, 1977, 1983.

LEBRON JAMES

LEBRON
JAMES

LeBron James was nervous. It was the 2006 NBA playoffs, and James, the NBA prodigy, was making his playoff debut with the Cleveland Cavaliers.

Everyone wanted to see how LeBron, who was nicknamed "King James," would handle the pressure of the playoffs. Game time. Two minutes and 23 seconds into the first quarter, James took his first shot—air ball!

No problem. Soon he was on his game. The "butterflies" disappeared. The Washington Wizards tried double-teaming James, to no avail. He waited and calmly passed the ball to teammates for open shots. James also created shots for himself.

By the end of the first half, he had scored 19 points, handed out seven assists, and picked off five rebounds. Chants of "MVP . . . MVP" by the Cleveland fans followed James.

By the end of the game, James had made history. With 32 points, 11 rebounds, and 11 assists, James had become only the third player to get a "triple-double" in his first playoff game.

"The only thing that surprised me was that it took LeBron 48 minutes to do it," Cavaliers guard Larry Hughes said after Cleveland's 97–86 first-round victory.[1]

James was a rarity: a player who jumped directly from high school to the NBA without playing a single second of college ball. He quickly became one of the NBA's most exciting players, helping fill arenas wherever he played. His number 23 uniform, a tribute to Michael Jordan, became one of the hottest selling items in arena gift shops. Before he even played his first pro game, James had already made history with a $90 million sneaker deal with Nike.

The 6-foot-8, 250-pound James is listed as a "small forward." But he is more than that—much more. He is an extremely agile player who can fit into the lineup at just about any position: point guard, scoring guard, rebounding forward, and scoring forward.

James was already a drawing card as a high school freshman, leading St. Vincent-St. Mary in Akron, Ohio, to a state championship. He won two more state titles, along with recognition as "Mr. Basketball" of Ohio three times, honoring the top high school player in the state.

James had developed a national reputation. His high school team was forced to move its practices to the University of Akron to accommodate all the media attention. And there was more—some of the NBA's top players, such as Shaquille O'Neal, showed up at LeBron's games, which in some cases were televised nationally.

LeBron continued to win awards after he turned pro—Rookie of the Year in 2003–04 and Most Valuable Player in the NBA All-Star Game among them.

Before LeBron put on the Cavs' wine and gold colors, the team had been shut out of the playoffs for seven straight years. In his first season, the Cavs were an immediate contender. By his third season in the league, the Cavaliers gained their first playoff appearance since 1998.

Spurred on by James, the Cavaliers won their first-round series against Washington before getting knocked out in the second. In 2007, James led the Cavs all the way to the Eastern Conference title and the NBA Finals for the first time in franchise history.

LEBRON JAMES

BORN: December 30, 1984, Akron, Ohio.

HIGH SCHOOL: St. Vincent-St. Mary, Akron, Ohio.

PRO: Cleveland Cavaliers (2003–present).

HONORS: 2003 Naismith Prep Player of the Year; 2004 NBA Rookie of the Year; 2006 NBA All-Star Game MVP; 2006 All-NBA First Team.

MICHAEL JORDAN

MICHAEL
JORDAN

What is the greatest Jordan moment?
It's hard to choose. First, there's the
Slam Dunk Contest during All-Star
Weekend in Chicago in 1988.

Jordan was up against "The Human Highli
Dominique Wilkins, in the final round. Wilki
first and put the pressure on Jordan. Wilki
had gained him the lead.

Jordan's heart sank, and the crowd groar
shot bounced off the back of the rim. There
one dunk left for both.

Suddenly a voice called from the crowd:
there and try it again. You can do it!"[1] It v
Erving, the player who had brought dunk s
spectacular new heights.[2]

Jordan was now sure of what to do. Just as he had done before, he dribbled down the court, tongue wagging. He pulled up at the foul line. Then "Air Jordan" leaped, floating toward the basket for what seemed like forever—just like Erving. Jordan extended his arm and jammed the ball through the basket. The Chicago Bulls' star was perfect this time. Winner of the slam-dunk contest: Michael Jordan!

Hard to top. But how about Jordan's performance in Game 5 of the 1997 NBA Finals—the contest known as the "Flu Game"? Before the game against Utah, Jordan sat at his locker in a weakened condition. He was sick with the stomach flu. How could he play in that condition? Somehow, Jordan summoned up his strength to score 38 points in 44 minutes. The Bulls beat the Jazz 90–88 on their way to another title.

Another performance hard to top. But how about the 1998 NBA Finals after Jordan came back from retirement? With 35 seconds left in Game 6, Jordan's Chicago Bulls trailed Utah, 86–83.

But, wait. It was time for Jordan to work his magic: He drove down court through the entire Jazz lineup and scored a basket to cut the Utah lead to one point. Then he stole the ball from Jazz forward Karl Malone. Again, he dribbled down court and this time pulled up for a jumper with 5.2 seconds left. Swish! The Bulls, behind their all-star guard's 45 points, pulled out an 87–86 victory for their sixth NBA championship.

"I didn't think he could top that game," Bulls coach Phil Jackson said of Jordan's performance in the 1997 Finals. "He topped it."[3]

Throughout his career, Jordan had made many buzzer-beating shots. As a freshman with the University of North Carolina, he hit the shot that won a national title. As a pro, Jordan's records speak for themselves. Among them: Six-time NBA champion with the Chicago Bulls; ten scoring titles; highest career scoring average of

30.12; five-time Most Valuable Player in the regular season, six MVP Finals awards, and a 14-time All-Star.

One more special moment to add to the long list of Jordan moments: It was April 20, 1986, only Jordan's second appearance in the playoffs and just his fifth playoff game. Facing a great Boston Celtics team, the youthful Jordan scored a playoff-record 63 points. Although the Bulls lost 135-131 in two overtimes, Jordan had put the rest of the NBA on notice. His time was coming. As Boston's Larry Bird said:

"Today, God was disguised as Michael Jordan."[4]

MICHAEL JORDAN

BORN: February 17, 1963, Brooklyn, New York.

. . . .

COLLEGE: University of North Carolina.

. . . .

PRO: Chicago Bulls, 1984–93 and 1995–98; Washington Wizards, 2001–03.

. . . .

RECORDS: Career points-per-game average (30.12); seasons leading league in total points (11); Finals MVP Awards (6).

. . . .

HONORS: Naismith College Player of the Year, 1984; USBWA College Player of the Year, 1984; NBA Rookie of the Year, 1985; NBA Most Valuable Player, 1988, 1991, 1992, 1996, 1998; NBA Finals MVP, 1991, 1992, 1993, 1996, 1997, 1998; NBA's 50th Anniversary All-Time Team; 2000 ESPY Athlete of the Century.

. . . .

SHAQUILLE O'NEAL

SHAQUILLE
O'NEAL

Could Shaquille O'Neal keep his promise? In 2004 O'Neal was traded from Los Angeles to Miami. He made a promise to Heat fans: an NBA championship.

In Shaq's first season in Miami, 2004–05, the Heat advanced to the Eastern Conference finals before losing to Detroit by a narrow margin in Game 7.

The Heat again faced the Pistons in the 2006 Eastern Conference finals and rushed to a 3–1 lead in the series. Suddenly O'Neal's game fell apart in Game 5 as the Heat lost.

"I got cursed out by Pat [Riley, the Heat coach], and my father," O'Neal said. "They told me I let it slip away."[1]

Game 6 presented a problem for the Heat. Dwayne Wade, the Heat's young star, had gone to the hospital right after the previous game suffering from the flu. With Wade only a shadow of himself in Game 6, the 7-foot-1, 320-pound Shaq prepared to put the team on his broad shoulders. Would he be successful?

He had always been motivated since his childhood as an "Army brat." His stepfather, Phillip A. Harrison, was assigned to Germany. On the Army base, O'Neal worked hard developing his basketball skills. Returning to the United States, O'Neal was enthusiastically greeted by the athletic director at Cole High School in San Antonio, Texas. O'Neal, on his way to becoming a 7-footer, eventually led Cole to the state championship.

O'Neal went on to Louisiana State University and reigned as one of the nation's premier collegiate big men. Shaq left school a year early as the No. 1 draft pick for the Orlando Magic, but not before he made a promise to his mother. He would return to school to get his degree. And he did.

Shaq's power game transformed the Magic from a losing team into a playoff contender. By Shaq's second season, he would lead Orlando to the NBA playoffs for the first time in club history. The next year, he led the Magic to the Finals.

One success followed another: Shaq won a gold medal at the 1996 Atlanta Olympics with the U.S. basketball team. He left the Magic to sign a seven-year contract worth $122 million with the Los Angeles Lakers. O'Neal was the centerpiece for Lakers championships in 2000, 2001, and 2002. He was voted MVP of the NBA Finals all three times.

A feud between O'Neal and Lakers' guard Kobe Bryant resulted in the big man leaving Los Angeles to join the Miami

Heat. Now it was time to answer the question: Could Shaq bring the championship he promised to Miami?

With a 3–2 series lead, the Heat only needed to win one of the next two games to dispose of the Pistons. With Wade obviously not at his best, Shaquille was put to the test. O'Neal carried some of the scoring load as the Heat took an early lead. When the Pistons closed to within seven points, O'Neal again took charge: He scored six straight points in two minutes, then led an 8–3 surge as the Heat took a 47–36 lead at the half.

With O'Neal pounding the boards and scoring key baskets, the Heat thwarted any chance of a Piston comeback. Shaq had scored 28 points, 16 rebounds, and blocked 5 shots in one of his best games of the season. The final: Miami 95, Detroit 78.

Shaq had delivered on his promise.

SHAQUILLE O'NEAL

BORN: March 6, 1972.

HIGH SCHOOL: Robert G. Cole Junior-Senior High School, San Antonio, Texas.

COLLEGE: Lousiana State University.

PRO: Orlando Magic, 1992–96; Los Angeles Lakers, 1996–2004; Miami Heat, 2005–08; Phoenix Suns, 2008–2009; Cleveland Cavaliers, 2009–present.

HONORS: 2000 NBA Most Valuable Player, three-time NBA Finals MVP, two-time All-Star MVP, 14-time All-Star.

HAKEEM OLAJUWON

HAKEEM
OLAJUWON

"Hakeem the Dream" was giving his opponents nightmares. It was the 1995 NBA playoffs. Olajuwon, the Houston Rockets' 7-foot center, was dominating the San Antonio Spurs.

Spinning left, Olajuwon hit an eight-footer. Then he spun right and connected on another eight-footer as he was falling out of bounds. He followed with a slam dunk. Then he sank an eighteen-foot jumper with his soft shooting touch!

Was this the same player who came to America from his native Nigeria in Africa with only a few months of basketball experience?

University of Houston basketball coach Guy Lewis was not sure the inexperienced new kid would fit in. Lewis wasn't expecting much. Olajuwon had played some games for the Nigerian national team.

In the closing seconds of one game, he caught a pass from a teammate. He leaped and tried to push the ball in the basket.

"I didn't know how to dunk," he said. "And I couldn't lay it up, either. I didn't know how to use the glass. I was so mad. We lost the game."[1]

Olajuwon's family expected him to come back to Nigeria and run the family cement business. He had other ideas. His dream was to be a professional basketball player.

Olajuwon, the hardest worker on the Cougar team, became a featured member of Houston's fearsome "Phi Slama Jama Fraternity." The Cougars, who gained the nickname for their fast-break basketball and ferocious dunk shooting, advanced to the NCAA finals two straight seasons.

Olajuwon left college after his junior year to pursue a dream and join the pros. He was the No. 1 pick in the 1984 NBA draft by the Houston Rockets, one of the worst teams in basketball.

Most centers in the NBA played with their backs to the basket. He was bored with that style of play. He wanted to get more movement into his game. Along with his feared dunk shot, he developed a cross-over dribble and a flair for scoring from unique angles. His footwork came naturally from his soccer background in Nigeria.

After ten years, Olajuwon won his first MVP trophy in the 1993–94 season. In a battle of superstar centers in the NBA Finals, Olajuwon outplayed Patrick Ewing to lead the Rockets over the New York Knicks for the league title.

Time for the 1995 playoffs. Olajuwon led the Rockets over Utah and Phoenix, two of the strongest teams in the league. That set up a showdown with the San Antonio Spurs, who had the best record during the regular season. The Spurs were led by league MVP David Robinson.

In Game 1 of the Western Conference finals series, Olajuwon scored 27 points along with eight rebounds and six assists. The Rockets upset the Spurs on their own court, 94–93, as Olajuwon assisted on the winning basket with 6.4 seconds left.

In Game 5, Olajuwon scored 42 points with nine rebounds and eight assists. Another upset on the Spurs court, 111–90. Game 6, another superb performance by the Houston star: 39 points and 17 rebounds as the Rockets wrapped up the series with a 100–95 victory.

"He was remarkable," Robinson said.[2]

The Rockets went on to win their second straight NBA title. Another dream season had come true for the Rockets, thanks to Hakeem.

HAKEEM OLAJUWON

BORN: January 21, 1963, Lagos, Nigeria.

COLLEGE: Houston.

PRO: Houston Rockets, 1984–2001; Toronto Raptors, 2001–2002.

HONORS: NBA Most Valuable Player, 1994; two-time Finals MVP, 1994–95; two-time NBA Defensive Player of the Year, 1993–94; six-time All-NBA First Team Selection, 1987–89, 1993–94, 1997; 12-time all-star, 1985–90, 1992–97; 1985 NBA All-Rookie Team; NBA's 50th Anniversary All-Time Team.

BILL RUSSELL

BILL
RUSSELL

It was a wintry night in Boston. The Boston Garden was packed to the rafters with Celtics fans. All eyes were on Bill Russell, the Celtics' star attraction in the 1960s.

He seemed to be everywhere at once. He swooped across the lane to block a shot. He altered another. Then Russell left his man and slid over to cover an opponent driving to the basket. He plucked a rebound off the backboard and fired an outlet pass to Bob Cousy. The Celtics were off and running.

It was something that Celtics fans had come to expect from the angular 6-foot-9 pivotman who won an incredible total of 11 NBA titles in 13 seasons.

It wasn't always this way. Can you believe that Russell, one of basketball's all-time greats, was cut from his junior high school team? In high school, he didn't stand out until his junior year. He didn't attract much attention from the colleges. He only received one offer—the University of San Francisco. Russell grabbed it.

In 1954, racism was rampant in America, and there were very few African-American players on college basketball teams. Dons coach Phil Woolpert was a forward thinker in starting three African-American players, Russell among them.

Russell led the Dons to consecutive national titles in 1955 and 1956. At one point, the Dons won 55 straight games—a record that stood until broken by UCLA in the 1970s.

Now it was time for the NBA. Russell's NBA career was impacted by the debut of Wilt Chamberlain with the Philadelphia Warriors in 1959. Their classic match-up was considered one of the greatest individual rivalries in the history of any sport. In their first meeting, Chamberlain outscored Russell 30–22. But Russell out-rebounded Chamberlain 35–28 to set the tone for a decade of spectacular clashes.

Chamberlain usually won the statistical battles. The Celtic star usually won the team championships. In the time they were in the league together, Russell won nine titles to Chamberlain's one. Russell's record against Chamberlain's teams: 86–57.

When the two met in the 1968 NBA playoffs, it was another clash of the titans. Russell's Celtics and Chamberlain's Philadelphia 76ers were tied 3–3 in the best-of-seven series. The Celtics had won two in a row. They were trying to become the first team in NBA history to come back from a 3–1 deficit.

The two rivals were fiercely competitive. Their match-ups usually came down to the final minutes when either big man would take over. With 34 seconds left, the Celtics held a 97–95 lead with Russell at the foul line for two shots. He made one, and Boston led 98–95. The 76ers took possession. Chet Walker drove for a basket. No way. Russell blocked his shot. Hal Greer took another shot for Philadelphia. It bounced off the rim. Russell was there to clear the rebound. Boston possession. The Celtics clinched the victory with two foul shots by Sam Jones. The Celtics were on their way to another league title.

By this time, Russell was handling the dual role of coach and player. He had become the first African-American head coach in any major American sport when he took over the job for the Celtics in 1966.

Now a player-coach, Russell continued to be a winner.

BILL RUSSELL

BORN: February 12, 1934, Monroe, Louisiana.

· ·

HIGH SCHOOL: McClymonds, Oakland, California.

· ·

COLLEGE: University of San Francisco.

· ·

PRO: Boston Celtics, 1956–69.

· ·

HONORS: Naismith Basketball Hall of Fame, 1975; five-time NBA Most Valuable Player, 1958, 1961, 1962, 1963, 1965; 12-time NBA All-Star; All-Star MVP, 1963; Olympic gold medalist, 1956.

· ·

DOMINIQUE WILKINS

DOMINIQUE
WILKINS

Dominique Wilkins prepared for the battle of his life. As he laced up his sneakers in the Atlanta Hawks' locker room, his mind was on the Boston Celtics.

It was the final game of their 1988 NBA Eastern Conference semifinals. It had come down to Game 7 and the continuing scoring battle between Wilkins, the so-called "Human Highlight Film", and the future Hall of Famer Larry Bird. And both were in a "zone." Like two great gunslingers from the Old West, they matched each other shot for shot. Neither could miss as the game headed toward its exciting finish.

Wilkins pulled out every shot in his arsenal—slam dunks, short-range jumpers, transition baskets, baskets off offensive rebounds, tip-ins. And Bird answered them with an array of shots of his own.

Wilkins had developed his basketball skills on the tough playgrounds in Baltimore, Maryland. He learned the playground code: If you want to shoot the ball, you have to get your hands on it. "So I started going up and getting it," Wilkins said. "I think it really helped. I was always playing with guys older than me."[1]

When he moved to Washington, North Carolina, with his family, Wilkins led the local high school to two straight state championships. There was a big battle among colleges to get his services. The University of Georgia finally won.

In college, Wilkins was regarded as a "swooper"—a classic small forward who worked 12 to 15 feet from the basket. His vertical jump was a phenomenal 47 inches! Wilkins left Georgia for the pros in 1982 after his junior year.

Wilkins always loved high-pressure situations. He liked competing in the Slam Dunk Contest at All-Star games. (He won two of them.) And he liked playing against the NBA's best, such as Bird.

It was crunch time in their 1988 playoff battle. Game Seven—winner take all. The teams took turns taking the lead. Neither could open a lead of more than seven points. With 1:43 left, Boston led 112–105. Back came Wilkins. He hit a basket, then two free throws, to cut the Celtics' lead to three points with 47 seconds remaining.

Boston still led 118–115 in the final seconds. Wilkins went to the foul line for two free throws. He made the first, then purposely missed the second hoping that a teammate could grab the rebound for a two-pointer to tie the game. No such luck—The Celtics rebounded and held on for a 118–116 decision. Boston had won despite an heroic effort by Wilkins, who outscored Bird 47–34.

Four years later, Wilkins hit the lowest point of his career when he suffered an injury to his Achilles tendon. In the days after the surgery with the cast still on, he was doing ninety-minute workouts. When the cast came off, his workouts intensified through long months of rehabilitation. He was determined to come back. He did, with one of his best pro seasons.

"I've always been a scorer," Wilkins said, "but it took some time before I knew that being a more complete player was more important." He was honored by several sports publications as the NBA Comeback Player of the Year in 1992–93.[2]

DOMINIQUE WILKINS

BORN: January 12, 1960, Paris, France.

HIGH SCHOOL: Washington High School, in Washington, North Carolina.

COLLEGE: University of Georgia, 1979–82.

PRO: Atlanta Hawks, 1982–94; Los Angeles Clippers, 1994; Boston Celtics, 1994–95; San Antonio Spurs, 1996–97; Orlando Magic, 1999.

HONORS: NBA All-Star Slam Dunk Champion, 1985, 1990; 1985–86 NBA scoring champion (30.3); NBA All-Rookie Team, 1983; All-NBA First Team, 1986; nine-time NBA All-Star; Naismith Basketball Hall of Fame, 2006.

CHAPTER NOTES

CHAPTER 1. KAREEM ABDUL-JABBAR

1. George Vecsey, "It's Historic, Just Like '55," *New York Times*, June 10, 1985, p. C1.

CHAPTER 2. VINCE CARTER

1. Gary Gramling, "Grand Slams," *Sports Illustrated for Kids*, March 2006, pp. 24–30.
2. Ibid.
3. Ibid.
4. Chis Sheridan, "Dunk Described as One of the Best Ever", Associated Press, September 25, 2000.

CHAPTER 3. DARRYL DAWKINS

1. Thomas Rogers, "Sports World Specials," *New York Times*, November 19, 1979, p. C2.
2. Chuck O'Donnell, "A Sweet Shattering," *Basketball Digest*, November/December 2004, pp. 18–19.
3. Ibid.
4. Ibid.

CHAPTER 4. JULIUS ERVING

1. Interview in the *Boston Globe*, n.d., <http://hoopedia.nba.com/index.php?title=Julius_Erving> (September 23, 2009).

CHAPTER 5. LEBRON JAMES

1. Tom Withers, "LeBron James Soars in First Playoff Game," The Associated Press, April 23, 2006.

CHAPTER 6. MICHAEL JORDAN

1. Chuck O'Donnell, "When the Knees Were Young," *Basketball Digest*, February 2003.
2. Ibid.
3. Mitch Lawrence, "Memories of MJ's First Two Acts," *ESPN*, September 10, 1999, <http://static.espn.go.com/nba/columns/lawrence_mitch/1250345.html> (September 23, 2009).
4. Ibid.

Chapter 7. SHAQUILLE O'NEAL

1. Jonathan Feigen, "Heat Finally Make Finals," the *Houston Chronicle*, June 3, 2006.

Chapter 8. HAKEEM OLAJUWON

1. Kevin Sherrington, "Rough-Edged Olajuwon Leaps Into Prominence," *The Sporting News 1983-84 Basketball Yearbook*, pp. 113–114.
2. Clifton Brown, "Rockets Do Homework and Return to Finals," *New York Times*, June 2, 1995, p. B7.

Chapter 10. DOMINIQUE WILKINS

1. Jack McCallum, "The Top Dog of Dunk," *Sports Illustrated*, November 30, 1981.
2. Roy Johnson, "If You've Got It, Flaunt It," *New York Times*, February 9, 1986, p. S1.

FURTHER READING

Basketball Top 10. New York: DK Publishing, 2004.

Kramer, Sydelle. *Basketball's Greatest Players*. New York: Random House, 1997.

INTERNET ADDRESSES

Official NBA Site
http://www.nba.com/

The Naismith Memorial Basketball Hall of Fame
http://www.hoophall.com/